Easy WEEKEND QUILTS

Martingale
Create with Confidence

Easy Weekend Quilts
© 2013 by Martingale & Company®

Martingale®
19021 120th Ave. NE, Ste. 102
Bothell, WA 98011-9511 USA
ShopMartingale.com

Printed in China
18 17 16 15 14 13   8 7 6 5 4 3 2 1

**Library of Congress Cataloging-in-Publication Data
is available upon request.**

ISBN: 978-1-60468-393-6

Mission Statement
Dedicated to providing quality products and service
to inspire creativity.

Credits
PRESIDENT AND CEO: Tom Wierzbicki
EDITOR IN CHIEF: Mary V. Green
DESIGN DIRECTOR: Paula Schlosser
MANAGING EDITOR: Karen Costello Soltys
ACQUISITIONS EDITOR: Karen M. Burns
COPY EDITOR: Melissa Bryan
PRODUCTION MANAGER: Regina Girard
COVER AND INTERIOR DESIGNER: Connor Chin
PHOTOGRAPHER: Brent Kane
ILLUSTRATORS: Adrienne Smitke, Laurel Strand,
    and Robin Strobel

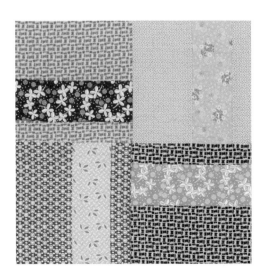

Contents

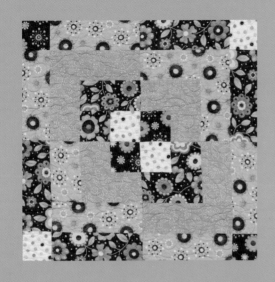

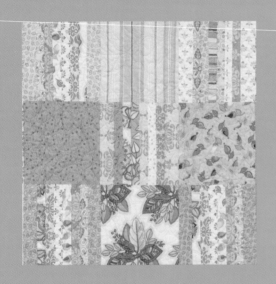

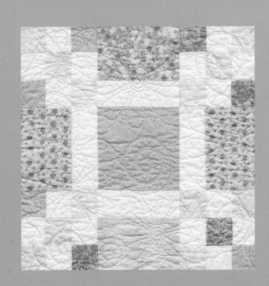

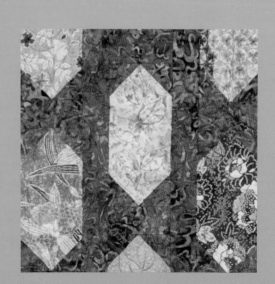

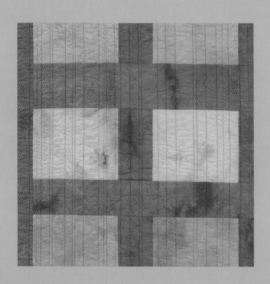

Introduction

You have a wide-open weekend coming up with nothing on your schedule: no chores to do, no errands to run, nowhere you need to be, nothing to do but . . . sew. Ah, bliss! Or maybe you're planning a quilt retreat, a few days of uninterrupted stitching time with your best friends. What a fun thing to look forward to!

Nearly as much fun as the quilting itself is the planning. What project will you make? Will it be a fat-quarter quilt, a quick strippy design, a scrap quilt? Will you dive into your stash or will there be a shopping trip involved?

Whether your quilt is destined to be a gift, a cozy cuddler for the back of the sofa, or a donation to a favorite charity, you'll find the ideal pattern in these pages. Many of the projects use precut fabrics, so you can get right to the sewing. And all of the projects are generously sized for use as lap or bed quilts.

So browse through the patterns, choose a color scheme, and gather your fabrics and tools. These bright, breezy designs were chosen with easy, stress-free sewing in mind, the kind of stitching that's ideal for a relaxing weekend. TGIF!

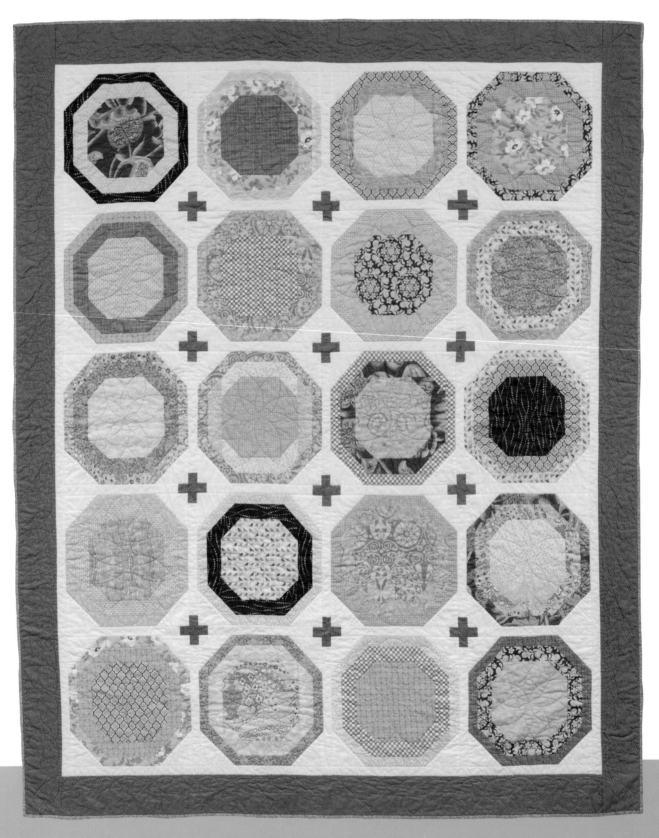

Designed by Adrienne Smitke; pieced by Judy Smitke and Adrienne Smitke;
machine quilted by Karen Burns of Compulsive Quilting

Quilt size: 65½" x 79½"
Block size: 13" x 13"

Confectionery

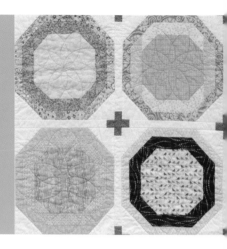

Adrienne's inspiration for this quilt came from those "everything-retro-is-cool-again" crocheted granny-square afghans, but the finished quilt reminded her more of candy! Bright, colorful jawbreakers; gumballs; and, Everlasting Gobstoppers, which change colors as you suck on them.

Pick your own scrappy palette of fat quarters and follow the cutting diagram carefully, because this clever quilt doesn't waste an inch of fabric!

aterials

Yardage is based on 42"-wide fabric. Fat quarters are 18" x 21".

20 fat quarters in a variety of colors for blocks

2 yards of white solid or print for sashing and inner border

1¼ yards of gray solid or print for sashing and outer border

⅝ yard of teal fabric for binding

4 yards of fabric for backing

71" x 85" piece of batting

utting

From *each* of the fat quarters, use the cutting diagram, right, to cut*:
1 square, 8½" x 8½"
2 strips, 2" x 8½"
2 strips, 2" x 11½"
4 squares, 2½" x 2½"
2 strips, 1½" x 11½"
2 strips, 1½" x 13½"
4 squares, 3½" x 3½"

From the white fabric, cut:
80 squares, 4" x 4"
17 strips, 1½" x 11½"
14 strips, 1½" x 12½"
7 strips, 1½" x 42"

From the gray fabric, cut:
24 squares, 1½" x 1½"
12 rectangles, 1½" x 3½"
7 strips, 4½" x 42"

From the teal fabric, cut:
8 strips, 2¼" x 42"

*Refer to the first part of the cutting diagram to cut each of the 20 fat quarters into the strips shown. Cut the strips into pieces for the blocks as shown in the second part of the diagram. Organize the pieces into sets based on their dimensions.

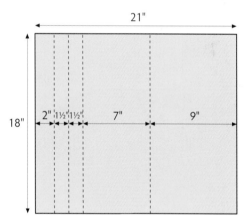

Cut into strips.

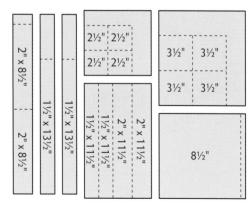

Cut strips into remaining pieces as shown.

7

Making the Blocks

1 Mark a diagonal line from corner to corner on the wrong side of four 2½" squares for the block inner ring. Sew the squares to a different-colored 8½" center square as shown. Trim and press the seam allowances toward the corners.

2 Sew 2" x 8½" strips that match the corner squares in step 1 to both sides of the unit. Press the seam allowances away from the block center. Sew matching 2" x 11½" strips to the top and bottom of the unit. Press.

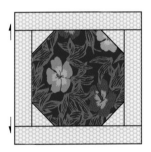

3 Using four 3½" squares in a different color, repeat step 1.

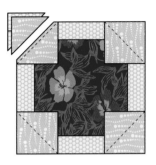

4 Sew matching 1½" x 11½" strips to the sides of the block. Press the seam allowances away from the block center. Sew matching 1½" x 13½" strips to the top and bottom of the block. Press.

5 With four white 4" squares, repeat step 1. Make 20 blocks.

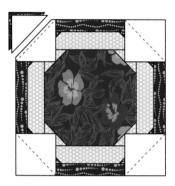

Making the Sashing

1 Sew a gray 1½" square to the end of a white 12½"-long strip. Make six. Sew a gray 1½" square to each end of a white 11½"-long strip. Make nine. For both sets of sashing strips, press the seam allowances toward the gray squares.

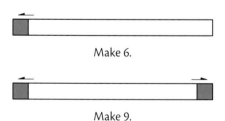

Make 6.

Make 9.

2 To make the sashing rows, sew two white 12½"-long strips, two white 11½"-long strips, and three gray 1½" × 3½" rectangles end to end as shown. Press the seam allowances toward the gray rectangles. Make four rows.

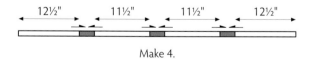

12½"   11½"   11½"   12½"

Make 4.

3 Find the center of each gray rectangle by folding it in half, and mark the center with a pin.

Assembling the Quilt Top

1 Sew four blocks and three matching sashing strips into rows to make two top/bottom rows with single gray squares in the sashing strips and three center rows with gray squares at both ends of the sashing strips. Press the seam allowances toward the blocks.

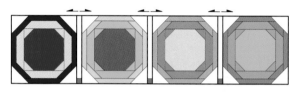

Top/bottom row.
Make 2.

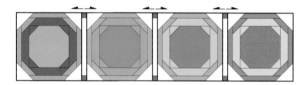

Center row.
Make 3.

2 Mark the centers of the gray squares in the sashing of the block rows with pins.

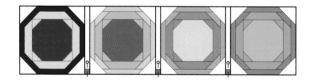

3 Arrange the block rows and sashing rows as shown.

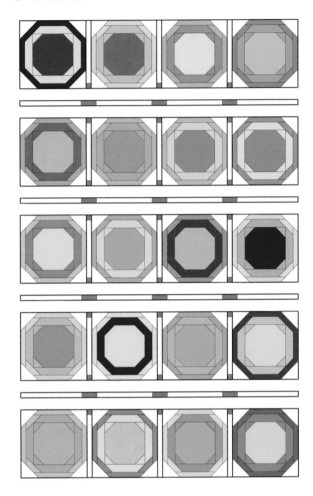

4 Sew the rows together, matching the centers of the gray squares in the block rows with the centers of the gray rectangles in the sashing rows. Press the seam allowances in one direction.

Adding the Borders

1 Join the white 1½" × 42" strips end to end to make one long strip. Cut two inner-border strips, 69½" long, and sew them to the sides of the quilt top. Press the seam allowances toward the inner borders. Cut two inner-border strips, 57½" long, and sew them to the top and bottom. Press the seam allowances toward the inner borders.

2 Join the gray 4½" × 42" strips end to end to make one long strip. Cut two outer-border strips, 71½" long, and attach them to the sides of the quilt top. Press the seam allowances toward the

outer borders. Cut two outer-border strips, 65½" long, and sew them to the top and bottom. Press the seam allowances toward the outer borders.

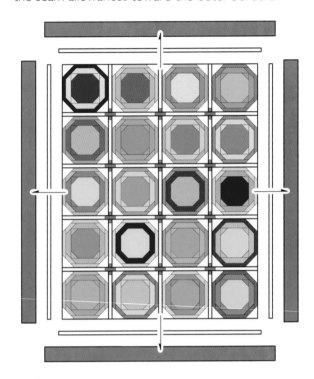

Finishing the Quilt

Go to ShopMartingale.com/HowtoQuilt for free downloadable information on any of the following steps.

1 Cut and piece the backing fabric so that it's about 6" larger than the quilt top.

2 Mark any quilting lines needed, and then layer the backing, batting, and quilt top. Baste the layers together and quilt as desired. The blocks in Adrienne's quilt were machine quilted in a pattern of concentric circles. The gray borders were quilted in whimsical loops.

3 Trim the excess batting and backing fabric even with the quilt top. Use the 2¼"-wide teal strips to make and attach double-fold binding.

4 Make and attach a quilt label.

Jack and Jill

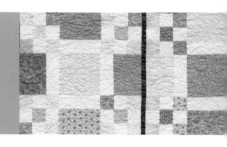

This quilt design is the perfect choice to use up those fat quarters you've collected. Divide your fat quarters into two color groups, add two neutral colors, and you'll be off and running to make a quilt for your lucky Jack or Jill!

Materials

Yardage is based on 42"-wide fabric. Fat quarters are 18" x 21".

2 yards of white solid for blocks

7 fat quarters of assorted pink fabrics for blocks

7 fat quarters of assorted green fabrics for blocks

1 yard of brown solid for sashing and binding

3⅝ yards of fabric for backing

64" x 78" piece of batting

Matching or invisible thread for appliqué

Choosing Jack or Jill

The materials, cutting, and assembly instructions are all based on making the pink "Jill" version of this project. To make a "Jack" quilt, simply substitute seven blue fat quarters for the pink ones, and then cut the blue fabrics as described for the pink ones.

Cutting

Cut strips across the width of the fabric unless otherwise specified. Cut fat quarters perpendicular to the selvage (20" long).

From the 7 pink fat quarters, cut a *total* of:
20 strips, 2" x 20"
11 strips, 5" x 20"; crosscut into:
    10 squares, 5" x 5"
    40 rectangles, 3½" x 5"

From the 7 green fat quarters, cut a *total* of:
20 strips, 2" x 20"
11 strips, 5" x 20"; crosscut into:
    10 squares, 5" x 5"
    40 rectangles, 3½" x 5"

From the white solid, cut:
16 strips, 2" x 42"; crosscut each strip into 2 strips, 2" x 20" (32 total)
4 strips, 5" x 42"; crosscut each strip into 20 rectangles, 2" x 5" (80 total)

From the brown solid, cut:
14 strips, 1" x 42"; crosscut 8 of the strips into 2 strips each, 1" x 14" (16 total; 1 is extra)
7 strips, 2½" x 42"

Making the Blocks

Sew a pink 2" x 20" strip to each long side of a white 2" x 20" strip to make a strip set. Press the seam allowances toward the pink strips. Make a total of eight strip sets. Cut each strip set into 10 segments, 2" wide (80 total).

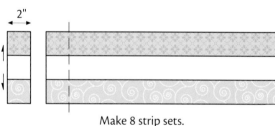

2"

Make 8 strip sets.
Cut 80 segments.

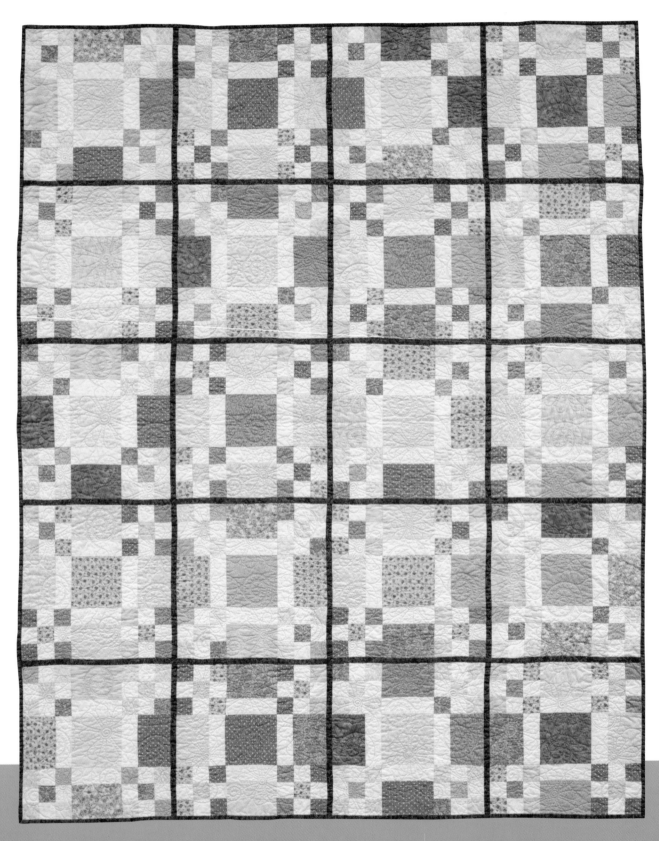

Designed and made by Jeanne Large and Shelley Wicks;
machine quilted by Colleen Lawrence

Quilt size: 56½" x 70"
Block size: 13½" x 13½"

2 Sew a white 2" × 20" strip to each long side of a pink 2" × 20" strip to make a strip set. Press the seam allowances toward the pink strip. Make a total of four strip sets. Cut each strip set into 10 segments, 2" wide (40 total).

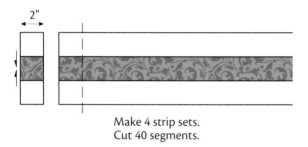

Make 4 strip sets.
Cut 40 segments.

3 Sew segments from step 1 to both sides of a segment from step 2 to make a nine-patch unit as shown. Press the seam allowances away from the center segment. Repeat to make 40 pink-and-white nine-patch units.

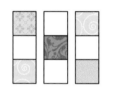

Make 40.

4 Repeat steps 1–3 using green and white 2" × 20" strips to make 40 green-and-white nine-patch units.

Make 40.

5 Sew a white 2" × 5" rectangle to one long edge of each pink 3½" × 5" rectangle. Repeat with the green 3½" × 5" rectangles. Press the seam allowances away from the white rectangles. Make 40 units in each color (80 total).

Make 40 each.

6 Arrange four pink nine-patch units, four green-and-white units from step 5, and a pink 5" square to form a block as shown. Sew the units into three rows, pressing the seam allowances as indicated. Sew the rows together and press toward the center row. Make 10 pink blocks.

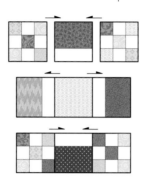 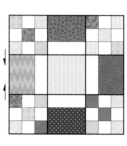

Make 10.

7 Repeat step 6 with the green nine-patch units, pink-and-white units from step 5, and green 5" squares to make 10 green blocks.

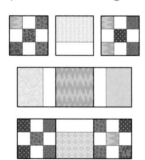 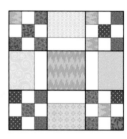

Make 10.

Assembling the Quilt Top

1 Lay out the blocks in five rows of four blocks each, alternating the color placement as shown.

2 Position the brown 1" × 14" sashing strips between the blocks in each row. Sew the blocks and sashing strips together into rows. Press the seam allowances toward the sashing strips.

3 Sew the remaining brown 1" × 42" strips end to end to make one continuous strip. From this length, cut four sashing strips, 56" long.

4 Sew the block rows and sashing strips together as shown. Press the seam allowances toward the sashing strips.

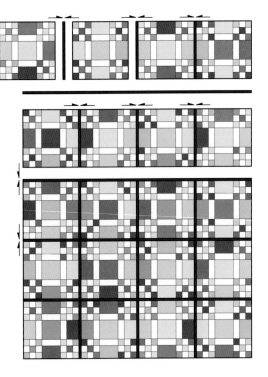

Finishing the Quilt

Go to ShopMartingale.com/HowtoQuilt for free downloadable information on any of the following steps.

1 Cut and piece the backing fabric so that it's about 6" larger than the quilt top.

2 Mark any quilting lines needed, and then layer the backing, batting, and quilt top. Baste the layers together and quilt as desired. The quilt shown features an allover floral design.

3 Trim the excess batting and backing fabric even with the quilt top. Use the 2½"-wide brown strips to make and attach double-fold binding.

4 Make and attach a quilt label.

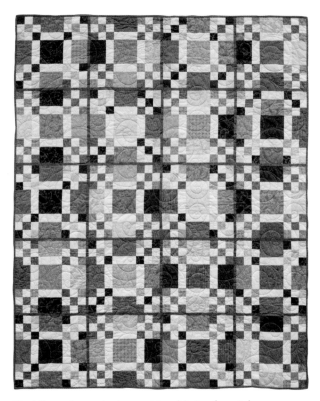

"Jack" version substitutes blue fabrics for pink.

Tutti Frutti for Mishayla

Claudia used a coordinating Moda Layer Cake and Honey Bun to achieve an instant scrappy look in this bright and charming quilt for her granddaughter Mishayla. Since most of the cutting was already done, the piecing was a breeze.

Materials

Yardage is based on 42"-wide fabric.

1 Honey Bun *or* 36 assorted print strips, 1½" × 42", for pieced blocks

1 coordinating Layer Cake *or* 36 assorted print squares, 10" × 10", for pieced blocks and alternate blocks

1⅝ yards of pink tone-on-tone print for border and binding

5 yards of fabric for backing

69" × 88" piece of batting

Cutting

From *each of 12* assorted print squares, cut:
4 rectangles, 2¼" × 10" (48 total)

From the pink tone-on-tone print, cut:
8 strips, 4" × 42"
8 strips, 2½" × 42"

Making the Blocks

1 Sort your 1½" × 42" strips into six sets of six strips each. Try to include lights and darks in each set to create some contrast and definition.

2 Sew six strips together lengthwise to make a strip set. Press all seam allowances in one direction. Make six strip sets.

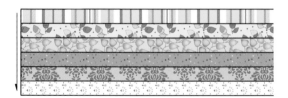

Make 6 strip sets.

3 Cut the strip sets into 10" lengths. By cutting carefully, you should get four strip-pieced segments from each strip set for a total of 24.

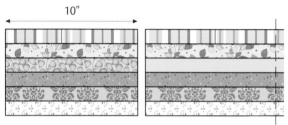

Cut 4 segments from each strip set.

4 Sew two matching 2¼" × 10" strips to each strip-pieced segment, one on each side as shown. Make 24.

Make 24.

Assembling the Quilt Top

1 Lay out the pieced blocks and the 24 remaining 10" squares in eight rows of six blocks each, alternating the pieced and plain blocks as shown.

2 Sew the blocks together into rows, pressing the seam allowances in alternate directions from row to row.

Designed and pieced by Claudia L'Heureux Cole;
machine quilted by Karen Burns of Compulsive Quilting

Quilt size: 64½" x 83½"
Block size: 9½" x 9½"

Tutti Frutti for Mishayla

3 Sew the rows together. Press the seam allowances in one direction.

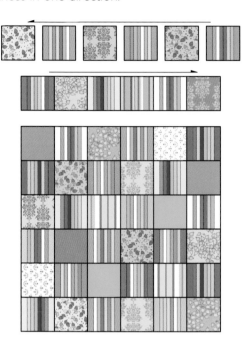

4 Measure the length of the quilt top through the center. Piece the 4"-wide pink border strips together end to end to make one long strip, and cut two strips to the length needed. Sew the borders to the sides of the quilt. Press the seam allowances toward the border. Measure the width of the quilt, including the borders just added, and cut two strips to the length needed. Sew the strips to the top and bottom of the quilt, and press the seam allowances toward the border.

Finishing the Quilt

Go to ShopMartingale.com/HowtoQuilt for free downloadable information on any of the following steps.

1 Cut and piece the backing fabric so that it's about 6" larger than the quilt top.

2 Mark any quilting lines needed, and then layer the backing, batting, and quilt top. Baste the layers together and quilt as desired.

3 Trim the excess batting and backing fabric even with the quilt top. Use the 2½"-wide pink strips to make and attach double-fold binding. To complete the binding entirely by machine, see the "Durable Binding" box below.

4 Make and attach a quilt label.

Durable Binding

After mending the hand-sewn binding on several quilts, Claudia has begun to use a machine-applied binding, especially for quilts that will be used a lot by her granddaughters.

Prepare the binding strips as usual, folding and pressing them in half lengthwise. Apply the folded binding to the back of the quilt just as you normally would attach it to the front. Fold the binding over the raw edges to the front of the quilt and stitch by machine as close to the edge as possible. If you're feeling extra clever, you can use one of the decorative stitches on your sewing machine for this final stitching.

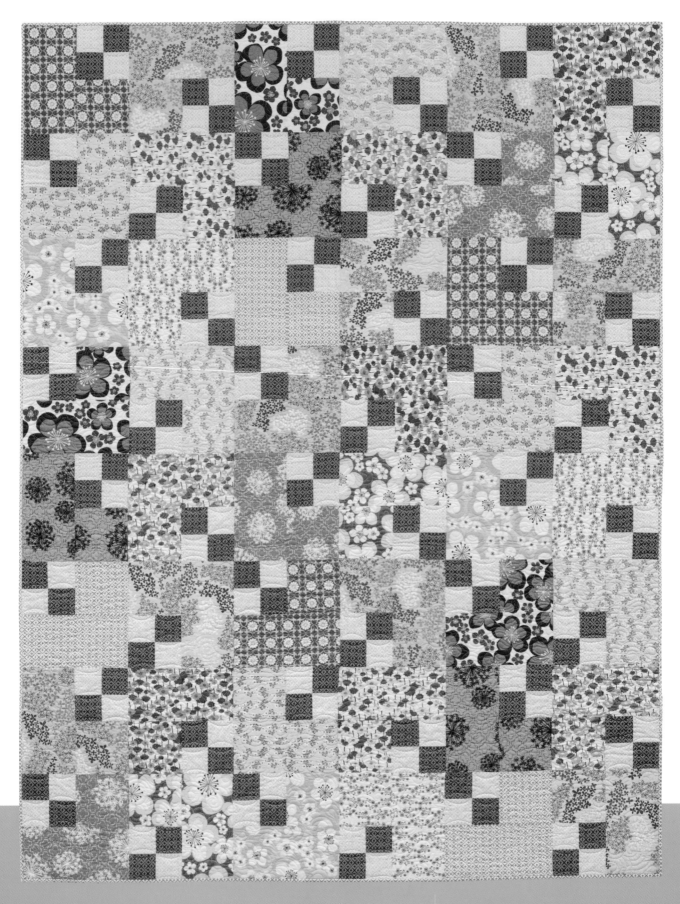

Pieced by Julie Herman; machine quilted by Angela Walters

Quilt size: 54½" x 72½"
Block size: 9" x 9"

Four-Patch Shift

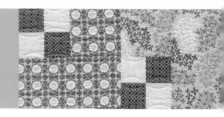

This enticing quilt puts a new spin on the basic four-patch unit. By rotating the four-patch placement in a larger block, the quilt design becomes playful and unexpected.

Materials

Yardage is based on 42"-wide fabric.

⅔ yard of pale-yellow print for four-patch units

⅔ yard of purple print for four-patch units

⅜ yard *each* of 16 assorted prints for blocks

⅝ yard of pale-green print for binding

3⅝ yards of fabric for backing

60" × 78" piece of batting

Cutting

From the pale-yellow print, cut:
    7 strips, 2¾" × 42"

From the purple print, cut:
    7 strips, 2¾" × 42"

From *each* of the 16 assorted prints, cut:
    2 strips, 5" × 42"; crosscut into:
        3 rectangles, 5" × 9½" (48 total)
        3 squares, 5" × 5" (48 total)

From the pale-green print, cut:
    7 strips, 2¼" × 42"

Making the Blocks

1 Sew a pale-yellow strip to the long side of a purple strip to make a strip set. Repeat to make a total of seven strip sets. Press the seam allowances open. Cut the strip sets into 96 segments, 2¾" wide.

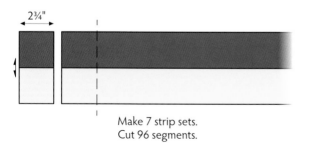

2¾"

Make 7 strip sets.
Cut 96 segments.

2 Sew two segments from step 1 together to make a four-patch unit. Press the seam allowances open. Make a total of 48 units.

Make 48.

3 Sew a four-patch unit to each print square, making sure to orient the colors in the four-patch exactly as shown. Press the seam allowances open.

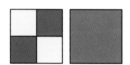 

Make 48.

4 Sew a matching rectangle to the bottom of each unit from step 3 to complete the block. Press the seam allowances open. Make a total of 48 blocks.

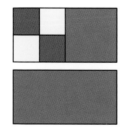 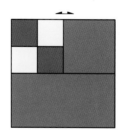

Make 48.

Assembling the Quilt Top

1 Lay out the blocks in eight rows of six blocks each as shown. In the odd-numbered rows, rotate the blocks so that the four-patch units are in the top-right and bottom-right corners. In the even-numbered rows, rotate the blocks so that the four-patch units are in the top-left and bottom-left corners.

2 Sew the blocks together into rows, pressing the seam allowances open.

3 Sew the rows together to complete the quilt top. Press.

Finishing the Quilt

Go to ShopMartingale.com/HowtoQuilt for free downloadable information on any of the following steps.

1 Cut and piece the backing fabric so that it's about 6" larger than the quilt top.

2 Mark any quilting lines needed, and then layer the backing, batting, and quilt top. Baste the layers together and quilt as desired.

3 Trim the excess batting and backing fabric even with the quilt top. Use the 2¼"-wide pale-green strips to make and attach double-fold binding.

4 Make and attach a quilt label.

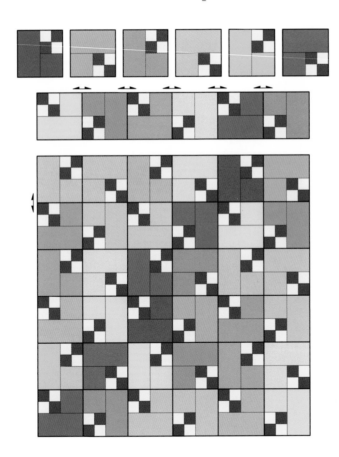

Knotted Squares

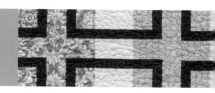

This bold and geometric quilt makes you stop and stare. Careful piecing yields fabulous results!

Materials

Yardage is based on 42"-wide fabric.

2¼ yards of green print for border

2 yards of white solid for blocks

1 Jelly Roll *or* 25 assorted print strips, 2½" × 42"

1⅓ yards of brown solid for blocks

⅝ yard of coral print for binding*

4½ yards of fabric for backing

78" × 78" piece of batting

You can use the remaining Jelly Roll strips for binding, if desired.

Cutting

If using a Jelly Roll, select 25 of the strips to use in the blocks.

From *each* of the 25 Jelly Roll strips or assorted print strips, cut:
- 1 rectangle, 2½" × 10½" (25 total)
- 2 rectangles, 2½" × 3½" (50 total)
- 1 rectangle, 2½" × 8½" (25 total)

From the white solid, cut:
- 27 strips, 2½" × 42"; crosscut into:
    - 25 rectangles, 2½" × 10½"
    - 100 squares, 2½" × 2½"
    - 100 rectangles, 2½" × 4½"

From the brown solid, cut:
- 28 strips, 1½" × 42"; crosscut into:
    - 100 rectangles, 1½" × 4½"
    - 100 rectangles, 1½" × 5½"

From the *lengthwise grain* of the green print, cut:
- 2 strips, 6½" × 60½"
- 2 strips, 6½" × 72½"

From the coral print, cut:
- 8 strips, 2½" × 42"

Making the Blocks

Amy pressed the seam allowances open in her blocks to make matching seams and sewing rows together during assembly easier.

1 Pin and sew a white 2½" × 10½" rectangle to a print 2½" × 10½" rectangle along the long side. Press the seam allowances open. Make 25 strip sets. Cut each strip set into four segments, 2½" wide, for a total of 100 segments.

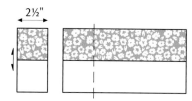

Cut 4 segments from each strip set.

2 Pin and sew a white 2½" × 4½" rectangle to each unit from step 1 as shown. Press the seam allowances open.

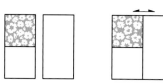

Make 100.

3 Pin and sew a brown 1½" × 4½" rectangle to each unit from step 2 as shown. Press the seam allowances open.

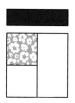

Make 100.

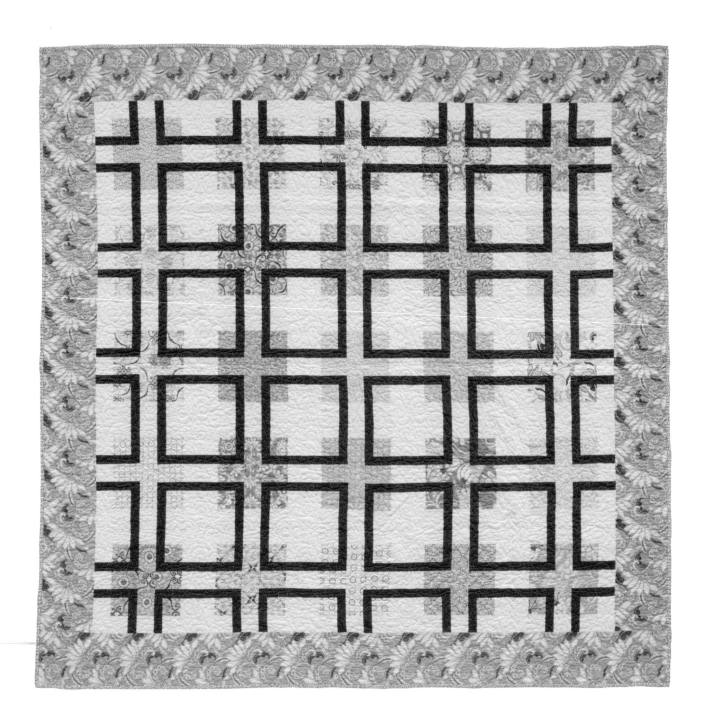

Designed and pieced by Amy Ellis;
quilted by Natalia Bonner

Quilt size: 72½" x 72½"
Block size: 12" x 12"

4 Pin and sew a brown 1½" × 5½" rectangle to each unit from step 3 as shown. Press the seam allowances open. Trim to 5½" square if necessary.

Make 100.

5 Pin and sew a white 2½" square to one end of a print 2½" × 3½" rectangle as shown. Press the seam allowances open. Make 50 units.

Make 50.

6 Pin and sew a white 2½" square to each end of a print 2½" × 8½" rectangle as shown. Press the seam allowances open. Make 25 units.

Make 25.

7 Pin and sew a unit from step 5 between two matching units from step 4, rotating the units as shown. Press the seam allowances open. Make 50 units.

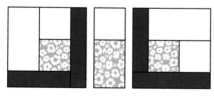
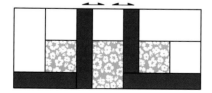

Make 50.

8 Pin and sew a unit from step 6 between two matching units from step 7 to make a block as shown. Press the seam allowances open. Make 25 blocks. Trim and square the blocks to 12½" × 12½".

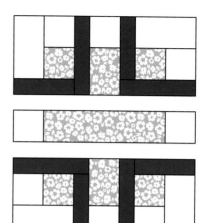

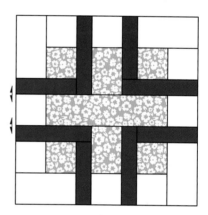

Make 25.

Assembling the Quilt Top

1 Lay out the blocks in five rows of five blocks each as shown.

2 Sew the blocks together into rows, pressing the seam allowances open.

3 Sew the rows together and press the seam allowances in one direction.

4 Pin and sew the 60½"-long green strips to the sides of the quilt top. Press the seam allowances toward the border. Pin and sew the 72½"-long green strips to the top and bottom of the quilt top. Press the seam allowances toward the border.

Finishing the Quilt

Go to ShopMartingale.com/HowtoQuilt for free downloadable information on any of the following steps.

1 Cut and piece the backing fabric so that it's about 6" larger than the quilt top.

2 Mark any quilting lines needed, and then layer the backing, batting, and quilt top. Baste the layers together and quilt as desired.

3 Trim the excess batting and backing fabric even with the quilt top. Use the 2½"-wide coral strips to make and attach double-fold binding.

4 Make and attach a quilt label.

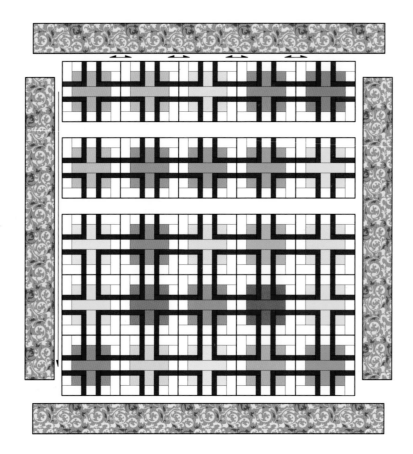

Square City

This quilt is ideal for featuring large-scale prints in the blocks and plain squares. Choose one neutral tone-on-tone print to help tie the whole design together.

Materials

Yardage is based on 42"-wide fabric. Fat quarters are 18" x 21".

25 fat quarters of assorted prints for pieced blocks and plain squares

1 yard of gray print for block centers

⅞ yard of large-scale striped fabric for bias binding

4⅜ yards of fabric for backing

73" x 73" piece of batting

Cutting

From the gray print, cut:
  5 strips, 6" x 42"; crosscut into 25 squares, 6" x 6"

From *each* of the 25 fat quarters, cut:
  1 square, 10" x 10" (25 total; 1 is extra)
  4 strips, 1½" x 18"; crosscut into:
    2 rectangles, 1½" x 10" (50 total)
    4 rectangles, 1½" x 8" (100 total)
    2 rectangles, 1½" x 6" (50 total)

From the large-scale striped fabric, cut:
  280" of 2¼"-wide bias binding

Making the Blocks

1 Sew matching print 1½" x 6" rectangles to opposite sides of a gray square. Press the seam allowances open.

2 Sew 1½" x 8" rectangles that match the rectangles in step 1 to the two remaining sides of the gray square. Press the seam allowances open.

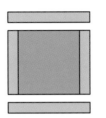 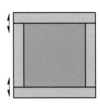

3 Sew matching print 1½" x 8" rectangles from a different fabric to opposite sides of the unit as shown. Press the seam allowances open.

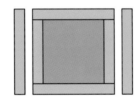 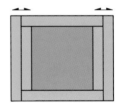

4 Sew 1½" x 10" rectangles that match the rectangles added in step 3 to the two remaining sides of the unit to complete the block. Press the seam allowances open. Repeat the process to make a total of 25 blocks.

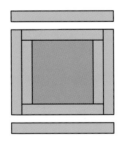 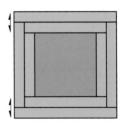

Make 25.

Pieced by Julie Herman;
machine quilted by Angela Walters

Quilt size: 67" x 67"
Block size: 9½" x 9½"

Assembling the Quilt Top

1 Lay out the blocks and the assorted 10" squares in seven rows of seven units each as shown, alternating the plain squares and the blocks in each row and from row to row.

2 Sew the blocks and squares together into rows; press the seam allowances open.

3 Sew the rows together to complete the quilt top. Press.

Finishing the Quilt

Go to ShopMartingale.com/HowtoQuilt for free downloadable information on any of the following steps.

1 Cut and piece the backing fabric so that it's about 6" larger than the quilt top.

2 Mark any quilting lines needed, and then layer the backing, batting, and quilt top. Baste the layers together and quilt as desired.

3 Trim the excess batting and backing fabric even with the quilt top. Use the striped 2¼"-wide strips to make and attach double-fold binding.

4 Make and attach a quilt label.

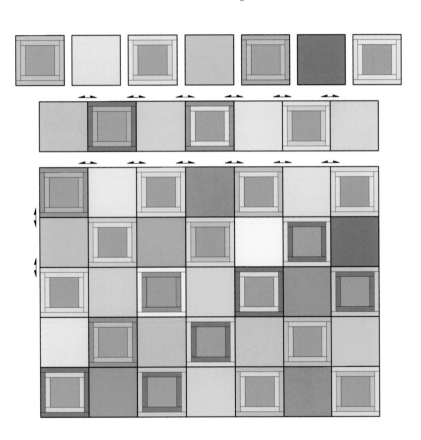

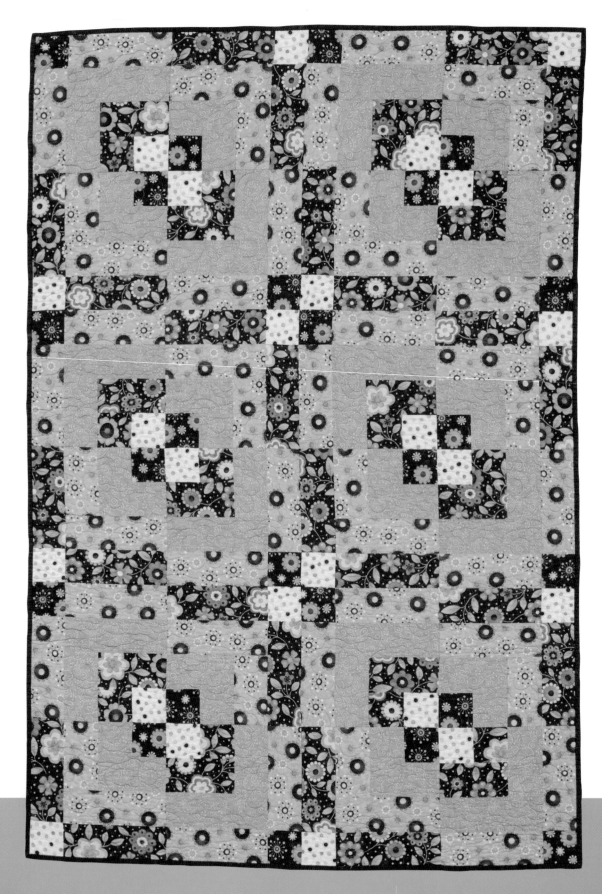

Designed and pieced by Amy Ellis;
machine quilted by Natalia Bonner

Quilt size: 48½" x 72½"
Block size: 12" x 12"

Modern V

Alternating blocks create a fun pattern within this quilt. Color placement is the key to this simple block. Look for saturated colors in your fabric choices for the best contrast.

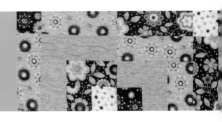

Materials

Yardage is based on 42"-wide fabric.

1¼ yards of green print for blocks

1⅛ yards of teal print for blocks

1⅛ yards of large-scale brown print for blocks

⅜ yard of medium-scale brown print for blocks

⅜ yard of cream print for blocks

⅝ yard of brown print for binding

4½ yards of fabric for backing

54" × 78" piece of batting

Cutting

From the green print, cut:
11 strips, 3½" × 42"; crosscut into:
   36 rectangles, 3½" × 9½", for pieces F, G, and M
   12 rectangles, 3½" × 6½", for piece L

From the teal print, cut:
8 strips, 3½" × 42"; crosscut into:
   24 rectangles, 3½" × 6½", for pieces D and K
   12 rectangles, 3½" × 9½", for piece E
   12 squares, 3½" × 3½", for piece J

From the large-scale brown print, cut:
9 strips, 3½" × 42"; crosscut into:
   12 squares, 3½" × 3½", for piece B
   12 rectangles, 3½" × 6½", for piece C
   24 rectangles, 3½" × 9½", for pieces N and O

From the medium-scale brown print, cut:
3 strips, 3½" × 42"; crosscut into 24 squares, 3½" × 3½", for pieces H and I

From the cream print, cut:
3 strips, 3½" × 42"; crosscut into 24 squares, 3½" × 3½", for pieces A and P

From the brown print for binding, cut:
7 strips, 2½" × 42"

Making the Blocks

1 Arrange the cut pieces in the block formation for block 1 and block 2 to keep all the pieces in order.

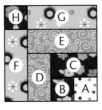
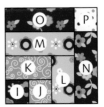

Block 1   Block 2

2 Pin and sew piece A to piece B, and piece I to piece J. Press the seam allowances as shown. Make 12 of each.

Make 12.

Make 12.

3 Pin and sew piece C to the A/B unit, and piece K to the I/J unit. Press the seam allowances as shown. Make 12 of each.

Make 12.

Make 12.

4 Pin and sew piece D to the A/B/C unit, and piece L to the I/J/K unit. Press the seam allowances as shown. Make 12 of each.

Make 12.

Make 12.

5 Pin and sew piece E to the A/B/C/D unit, and piece M to the I/J/K/L unit. Press the seam allowances as shown. Make 12 of each.

Make 12.

Make 12.

6 Pin and sew piece F to the A/B/C/D/E unit, and piece N to the I/J/K/L/M unit. Press the seam allowances as shown. Make 12 of each.

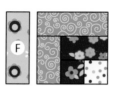 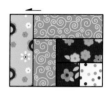

Make 12.

 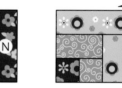

Make 12.

7 Pin and sew piece G to piece H, and piece O to piece P. Press the seam allowances as shown. Make 12 of each.

Make 12.

Make 12.

8 Pin and sew unit G/H to the A/B/C/D/E/F unit, and unit O/P to the I/J/K/L/M/N unit. Press the seam allowances as shown. Make 12 each of block 1 and block 2. Trim and square the blocks to 12½" × 12½".

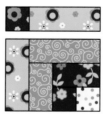 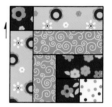

Block 1.
Make 12.

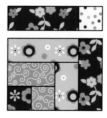 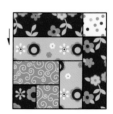

Block 2.
Make 12.

Assembling the Quilt Top

1. Lay out the blocks in six rows of four blocks each, alternating blocks 1 and 2 and orienting them as shown.

2. Sew the blocks together into rows, pressing the seam allowances in alternate directions from row to row.

3. Sew the rows together to complete the quilt top. Press the seam allowances in one direction.

Finishing the Quilt

Go to ShopMartingale.com/HowtoQuilt for free downloadable information on any of the following steps.

1. Cut and piece the backing fabric so that it's about 6" larger than the quilt top.

2. Mark any quilting lines needed, and then layer the backing, batting, and quilt top. Baste the layers together and quilt as desired.

3. Trim the excess batting and backing fabric even with the quilt top. Use the 2½"-wide brown strips to make and attach double-fold binding.

4. Make and attach a quilt label.

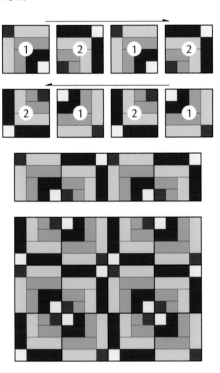

Designed and pieced by Amy Ellis;
machine quilted by Natalia Bonner

Quilt size: 58½" x 58½"

Graduation

This bold geometric quilt is made without constructing pieced blocks. Go right from cutting your pieces to assembling your quilt top. What could be easier?

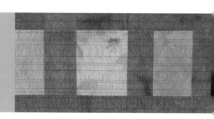

Materials

Yardage is based on 42"-wide fabric.

2½ yards of sienna solid for sashing and border

⅞ yard of brown solid for body and binding

⅔ yard of blue solid for quilt top

⅜ yard of gold solid for quilt top

⅜ yard of green solid for quilt top

¼ yard of cream solid for quilt top

3½ yards of fabric for backing

64" × 64" piece of batting

Cutting

From the blue solid, cut:
2 strips, 10½" × 42"; crosscut into 4 squares, 10½" × 10½"

From the gold solid, cut:
2 strips, 8½" × 42"; crosscut into 4 rectangles, 8½" × 10½"

From the green solid, cut:
2 strips, 6½" × 42"; crosscut into 4 rectangles, 6½" × 10½"

From the brown solid, cut:
2 strips, 4½" × 42"; crosscut into 4 rectangles, 4½" × 10½"
6 strips, 2½" × 42"

From the cream solid, cut:
2 strips, 2½" × 42"; crosscut into 4 rectangles, 2½" × 10½"

From the *crosswise grain* of the sienna solid, cut:
4 strips, 4½" × 42"; crosscut into:
3 rectangles, 4½" × 10½"
3 rectangles, 4½" × 8½"
3 rectangles, 4½" × 6½"
3 squares, 4½" × 4½"
3 rectangles, 2½" × 4½"

From the *lengthwise grain* of the remaining sienna solid, cut:
1 strip, 5½" × 52½"
1 strip, 4½" × 52½"
1 strip, 3½" × 52½"
1 strip, 2½" × 52½"
2 strips, 3½" × 44½"
2 strips, 7½" × 58½"

Oganizing Your Pieces

Binder clips from the office-supply store are a nice way to keep pieces together without using pins that little fingers can find. As an added bonus, you can slip a piece of paper under each clip to easily label the groups of pieces.

Assembling the Quilt Top

1 Pin and sew a sienna sashing rectangle to the appropriate-sized colored rectangle. Repeat for each of the remaining colored rectangles. Press the seam allowances as shown. Make three of each color.

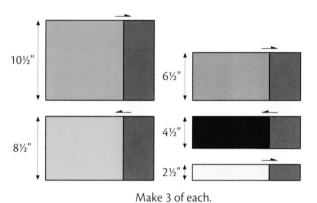

Make 3 of each.

2 Lay out three matching units from step 1 and a matching colored rectangle at the right end. Pin and sew the units together to make one row of blocks for each color. Press the seam allowances as shown.

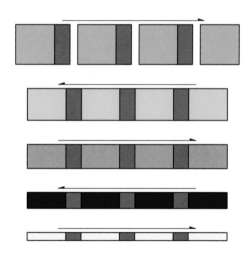

3 Pin and sew the blue 10½"-wide row to the 5½" × 52½" sashing strip. Press the seam allowances toward the sashing strip.

4 Pin and sew the gold 8½"-wide row to the 4½" × 52½" sashing strip. Press the seam allowances toward the sashing strip.

5 Pin and sew the green 6½"-wide row to the 3½" × 52½" sashing strip. Press the seam allowances toward the sashing strip.

6 Pin and sew the brown 4½"-wide row to the 2½" × 52½" sashing strip. Press the seam allowances toward the sashing strip.

7 Pin the cream 2½"-wide row to the bottom of the assembled row from step 6. To line up the seams, slide a long ruler between the layers, lay the edge of the ruler along the seam of one row of blocks, and line up the corresponding seam on the other row of blocks. Remove the ruler without moving the fabric, and pin in place. Sew the rows together. Press the seam allowances toward the sashing strip.

8 Lay out the rows as shown. Pin and sew them together, making sure to line up the seams. Press the seam allowances toward the sashing strips.

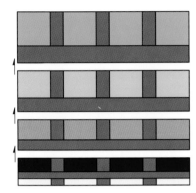

9 Pin and sew the 3½" x 44½" border strips to the quilt sides. Press the seam allowances toward the borders, and trim any excess. Pin and sew the 7½" x 58½" border strips to the top and bottom of the quilt. Press the seam allowances toward the borders, and trim any excess.

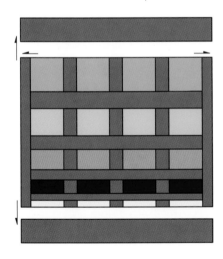

Finishing the Quilt

Go to ShopMartingale.com/HowtoQuilt for free downloadable information on any of the following steps.

1 Cut and piece the backing fabric so that it's about 6" larger than the quilt top.

2 Layer the backing, batting, and quilt top. Baste the layers together and quilt as desired. This quilt is very minimalistic, and straight lines of quilting add to the design. You don't even have to measure; add a line of quilting here and there and see what you think.

3 Trim the excess batting and backing fabric even with the quilt top. Use the brown 2½"-wide strips to make and attach double-fold binding.

4 Make and attach a quilt label.

Designed and pieced by Leanne Clare;
machine quilted by Karen Burns of Compulsive Quilting

Quilt size: 61" x 75½"
Block size: 3½" x 7½"

Emerald Forest

This quilt features a collection of beautiful Asian-print fat quarters. The addition of a brown batik pulls them all together and creates an aura of depth and lushness. You can start with any fabric collection that speaks to you, and choose one unifying color for the background.

Materials

Yardage is based on 42"-wide fabric. Fat quarters are 18" x 21".

8 assorted fat quarters for pieced blocks

4⅛ yards of brown batik for sashing and inner and outer borders

⅜ yard of light-green fabric for middle border

⅔ yard of dark-brown batik for binding

4⅝ yards of fabric for backing

67" x 82" piece of batting

Cutting

From *each* of the 8 fat quarters, cut:
  10 rectangles, 4" x 8" (80 total; 3 are extra)

From the brown batik, cut:
  19 strips, 2¼" x 42"; crosscut into 308 squares, 2¼" x 2¼"
  5 strips, 4" x 42"; crosscut into:
      11 squares, 4" x 4"
      66 rectangles, 2" x 4"
  24 strips, 2" x 42"
  7 strips, 3" x 42"

From the light-green fabric, cut:
  7 strips, 1½" x 42"

From the dark-brown batik, cut:
  8 strips, 2½" x 42"

Assembling the Quilt Top

1 Mark a diagonal line from corner to corner on the wrong side of all the 2¼" brown-batik squares. Place a square on each corner of a 4" x 8" rectangle, and stitch along the marked lines as shown. Trim the excess corner fabric, leaving a ¼" seam allowance. Press the seam allowances toward the corners. Make 77.

Make 77.

2 Piece together 17 of the 2"-wide brown-batik strips to form one long strip. From this length, cut 10 strips, 65½" long, for vertical sashing.

3 Lay out the blocks from step 1 in 11 vertical rows of seven blocks each, separated by 2" x 4" brown-batik rectangles. Add a vertical sashing strip between each row and offset the blocks as shown

by adding the 4" brown-batik squares to the top or bottom of each row. Rearrange the blocks as desired until you're satisfied with the color placement.

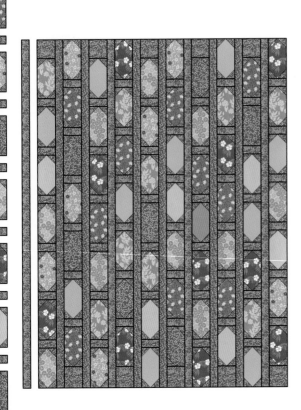

4 Sew the blocks, rectangles, and squares together into vertical rows. Press the seam allowances toward the sashing rectangles and squares.

5 Sew the rows together with the vertical sashing strips; press the seam allowances toward the vertical sashing.

Adding the Borders

1 Sew the remaining 2"-wide brown-batik strips together end to end to make one long strip. Measure the width of the quilt top through the center and cut two border strips to this length. Sew them to the top and bottom of the quilt. Press the seam allowances toward the border.

2 Measure the length of the quilt top through the center, including the borders just added, and cut two brown strips to this length. Sew the strips to the sides of the quilt, and press the seam allowances toward the border.

3 Repeat to add the 1½"-wide light-green strips for the middle border and the 3"-wide brown-batik strips for the outer border. Press all seam allowances toward the darker borders.

Finishing the Quilt

1 Cut and piece the backing fabric so that it's about 6" larger than the quilt top.

2 Mark any quilting lines needed, and then layer the backing, batting, and quilt top. Baste the layers together and quilt as desired.

3 Trim the excess batting and backing fabric even with the quilt top. Use the 2½"-wide dark-brown strips to make and attach double-fold binding.

4 Make and attach a quilt label.

Indonesian Railroad

This easy quilt is enhanced by the dimensional look and rich colors of the batik fabrics. One strip set will make four blocks. Simply crosscut the strip sets, rotate every other segment, and stitch them back together. You can make this quilt any size you want, from table topper to lap quilt to king size, like this one.

Materials

Yardage is based on 42"-wide fabric.

8⅞ yards *total* of assorted batiks for blocks

2⅝ yards of dark-blue print for blocks

2¼ yards of blue batik for border

⅞ yard of fabric for binding*

9¾ yards of fabric for backing

114" x 114" piece of batting

*You can use leftover strips of the assorted batiks, if desired, as Terry did.

Cutting

From the assorted batiks, cut a *total* of:
43 strips, 6½" x 42"

From the dark-blue print, cut:
43 strips, 2" x 42"

From the blue batik, cut:
11 strips, 6½" x 42"

From the binding fabric, cut:
11 strips, 2¼" x 42"

Making the Blocks

1 Sew a dark-blue strip to one long edge of each assorted batik strip. Make 43 strip sets. Press the seam allowances toward the blue strips. Crosscut each strip set into 20 segments, 2" wide. Stack the strip sets for quick cutting.

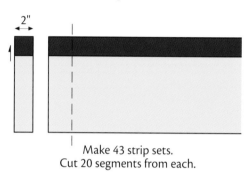

Make 43 strip sets.
Cut 20 segments from each.

2 Sew five identical segments together, rotating the segments as shown to make the design. Repeat to make a total of 169 blocks. You will have enough segments left over to make three additional blocks, if desired.

Make 169 total.

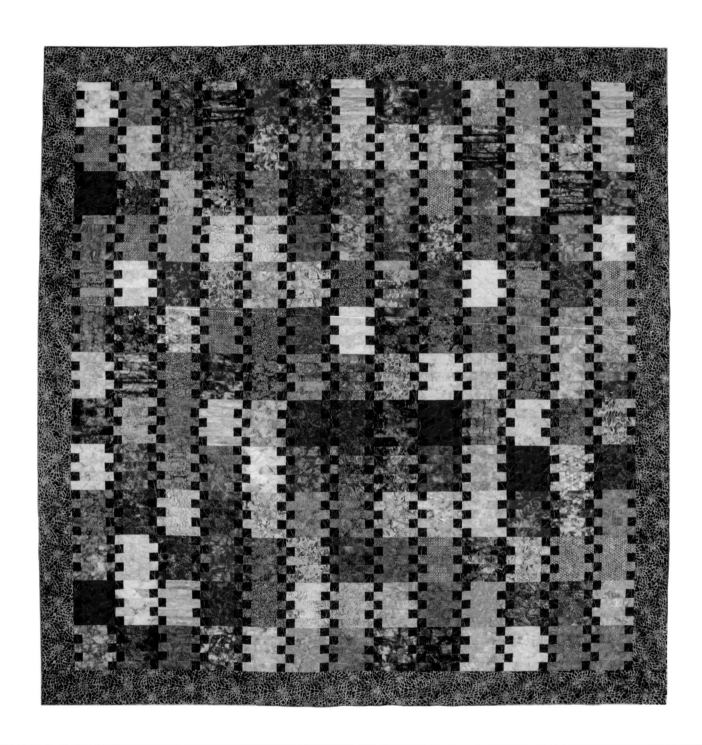

Designed and pieced by Terry Martin;
machine quilted by Adrienne Reynolds

Quilt size: 109½" x 109½"
Block size: 7½" x 7½"

Assembling the Quilt Top

1. Lay out the blocks in 13 rows of 13 blocks each as shown, making sure to alternate the placement of the dark-blue squares from row to row.

2. Sew the blocks together into rows. Press the seam allowances in alternate directions from row to row.

3. Sew the rows together. Press the seam allowances in one direction.

4. Measure the length of the quilt top through the center. Piece the 6½"-wide blue-batik strips together end to end to make one long strip, and cut two strips to the length needed. Sew the borders to the sides of the quilt. Press the seam allowances toward the border. Measure the width of the quilt top, including the borders just added, and cut two strips to the length needed. Sew the strips to the top and bottom of the quilt, and press the seam allowances toward the border.

Finishing the Quilt

Go to ShopMartingale.com/HowtoQuilt for free downloadable information on any of the following steps.

1. Cut and piece the backing fabric so that it's about 6" larger than the quilt top.

2. Mark any quilting lines needed, and then layer the backing, batting, and quilt top. Baste the layers together and quilt as desired.

3. Trim the excess batting and backing fabric even with the quilt top. Use the 2¼"-wide binding strips to make and attach double-fold binding.

4. Make and attach a quilt label.

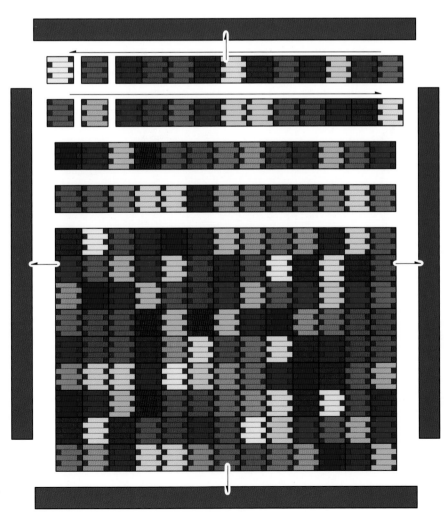

Quilt assembly

Designed and pieced by Amy Ellis;
machine quilted by Natalia Bonner

Quilt size: 72½" x 96½"
Block size: 12" x 12"

1, 2, 3!

Mix up your prints—two per block—for a fantastic scrappy look in your quilt. This quilt goes together in a snap. Instructions are given for a twin-size quilt; see optional fabric requirements for a baby quilt and a lap quilt.

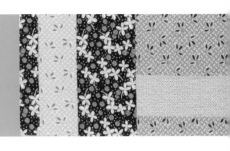

Materials

Yardage is based on 42"-wide fabric.

½ yard *each* of 16 assorted prints for blocks

¾ yard of fabric for binding*

5¾ yards of fabric for backing

78" × 102" piece of batting

You can use leftover strips cut from prints for the blocks, if desired, as Amy did.

Optional Quilt Sizes

Baby Quilt

For a baby quilt, piece 12 blocks to make a 36½" × 48½" quilt. You'll need:

   ½ yard *each* of 4 assorted prints for blocks
   ½ yard of fabric for binding
   1½ yards of fabric for backing
   42" × 54" piece of batting

Lap Quilt

For a lap quilt, piece 30 blocks for a 60½" × 72½" quilt. You'll need:

   ½ yard *each* of 10 assorted prints for blocks
   ⅝ yard of fabric for binding
   4 yards of fabric for backing
   66" × 78" piece of batting

Cutting

From *each* of the 16 assorted prints, cut:
   1 strip, 6½" × 42"; crosscut into 3 rectangles, 6½" × 12½" (48 total), for piece C
   1 strip, 4½" × 42"; crosscut into 3 rectangles, 4½" × 12½" (48 total), for piece B
   1 strip, 2½" × 42"; crosscut into 3 rectangles, 2½" × 12½" (48 total), for piece A

From the binding fabric, cut:
   9 strips, 2½" × 42"

Making the Blocks

Each block is made of matching A and C pieces, with a contrasting B piece sandwiched in between. Amy recommends taking the time to plan out combinations you like best for each block before starting to sew.

1   Pin and sew piece A to piece B. Press the seam allowances toward piece B. Make 48 units.

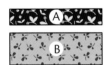 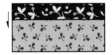

Make 48.

2   Pin and sew piece C (matching piece A) to the bottom of the A/B unit. Press the seam allowances toward piece C. Make 48 blocks. Trim and square the blocks to 12½" × 12½".

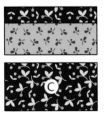 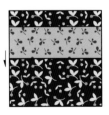

Make 48.

Assembling the Quilt Top

1 Lay out the blocks in eight rows of six blocks each, orienting the blocks as shown. Take your time balancing the colors within the quilt top.

2 Sew the blocks together into rows, pressing the seam allowances in alternate directions from row to row.

3 Sew the rows together to complete the quilt top. Press the seam allowances in one direction.

Finishing the Quilt

Go to ShopMartingale.com/HowtoQuilt for free downloadable information on any of the following steps.

1 Cut and piece the backing fabric so that it's about 6" larger than the quilt top.

2 Mark any quilting lines needed, and then layer the backing, batting, and quilt top. Baste the layers together and quilt as desired.

3 Trim the excess batting and backing fabric even with the quilt top. Use the 2½"-wide binding strips to make and attach double-fold binding.

4 Make and attach a quilt label.

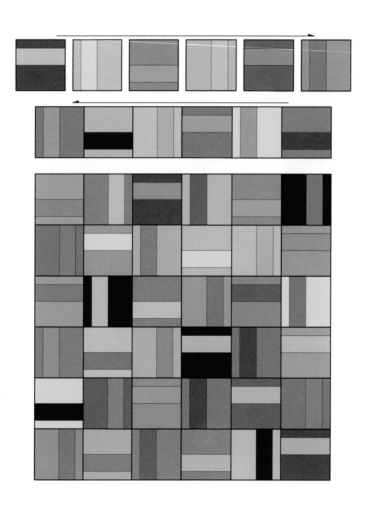

Rows of Bricks

This quilt is ideal for large-scale, stunning prints that need a place to shine. Here, rows of cool-colored bricks are stacked on wide strips of a neutral gray print. But this design will work equally well with hot and spicy colors.

Materials

Yardage is based on 42"-wide fabric.

¼ yard *each* of 19 assorted bright prints for horizontal rows

1⅞ yards of gray print for horizontal bars and binding

5 yards of fabric for backing*

63" × 81" piece of batting

*If your backing fabric measures a true 42" wide after trimming off the selvages, you'll need only 3⅞ yards.

Cutting

From *each of 8* assorted bright prints, cut:
  1 strip, 5" × 42"; crosscut into:
    3 rectangles, 5" × 10" (24 total)
    1 rectangle, 5" × 5¼" (8 total)

From *each of the remaining 11* assorted bright prints, cut:
  1 strip, 5" × 42"; crosscut into 4 rectangles, 5" × 10" (44 total)

From the *lengthwise grain* of the gray print, cut:
  3 strips, 7½" × 57½"
  5 strips, 2¼" × 57"

Making the Rows

1 Sew six assorted 5" × 10" rectangles end to end to make a row. Press the seam allowances open. Make eight rows.

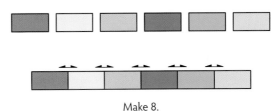

Make 8.

2 Sew five assorted 5" × 10" rectangles end to end to make a row. Sew a 5" × 5¼" rectangle to each end to complete the row. Press the seam allowances open. Make four of these rows.

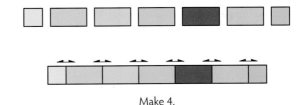

Make 4.

3 Sew a row from step 1 to each long side of a row from step 2 to complete a pieced section. Press the seam allowances open. Make four pieced sections.

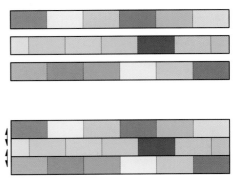

Make 4.

Pieced by Julie Herman;
machine quilted by Angela Walters

Quilt size: 57½" x 75½"

Assembling the Quilt Top

1. Lay out the four pieced sections and the gray 7½"-wide strips, alternating them as shown.

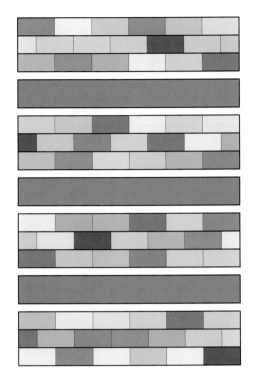

2. Sew the sections and strips together to complete the quilt top. Press the seam allowances open.

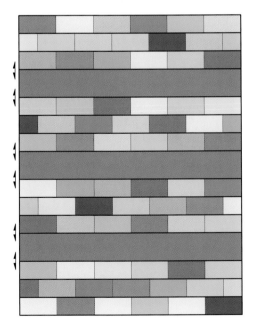

Finishing the Quilt

Go to ShopMartingale.com/HowtoQuilt for free downloadable information on any of the following steps.

1. Cut and piece the backing fabric so that it's about 6" larger than the quilt top.

2. Mark any quilting lines needed, and then layer the backing, batting, and quilt top. Baste the layers together and quilt as desired.

3. Trim the excess batting and backing fabric even with the quilt top. Use the gray 2¼"-wide strips to make and attach double-fold binding.

4. Make and attach a quilt label.

If you've enjoyed the projects in this book, look for these other books by the project designers. Ask for them at your local quilt shop, or go to ShopMartingale.com.

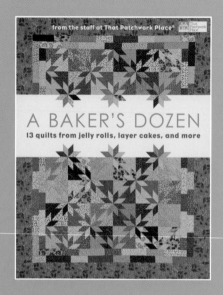

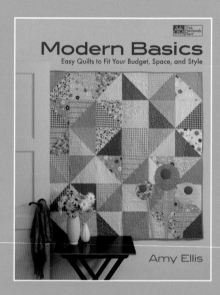

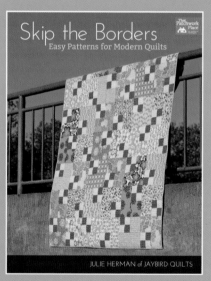

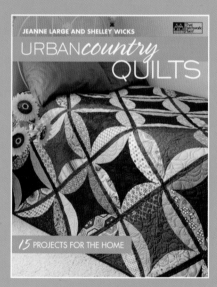

What's your creative passion?

Find it at **ShopMartingale.com**

books • eBooks • ePatterns • daily blog • free projects
videos • tutorials • inspiration • giveaways